FLOWERS:
The Language of Artists & Poets

KRISTEN CLARK

KRISTEN CLARK

Published by American Mutt Press, a division of The Communication Leader, LLC.

No part of this publication may be reproduced, stored in a retrieval system or transmitted in any form or by any means, electronic, mechanical, photocopying, recording or otherwise, without the written permission of the publisher.

Compiled and edited by Kristen Clark with American Mutt Press.

Photographs courtesy of various artists, with their permission and compliments.

Copyright © 2015 American Mutt Press

All rights reserved.

ISBN-13: 978-1943470013
ISBN-10: 1943470014

Poetry is the silence and speech between
a wet struggling root of a flower
and a sunlit blossom of that flower.

Carl Sandburg

FEATURED POEMS

A Few Introductory Words	13
God Made a Little Gentian *Emily Dickinson*	19
Easter Flower *Claude McKay*	20
The Primrose *Thomas Carew*	21
Daisy *Francis Thompson*	22
We Should Not Mind So Small A Flower *Emily Dickinson*	27
The Sick Rose *William Blake*	28
The Wild Honey-Suckle *Philip Freneau*	29
The Tuft of Flowers *Robert Frost*	33
The Goddess in the Wood *Rupert Brooke*	36
The Bluebell *Anne Bronte*	37

The Rose   41
William Browne

Litanies of the Rose   42
Remy De Gourmont

The Death of the Flowers   43
William Cullen Bryant

The Flower Must Not Blame the Bee   46
Emily Dickinson

Fancy   49
John Keats

A Tulip Garden   55
Amy Lowell

Asking for Roses   56
Robert Frost

To the Same Flower (Second Poem)   58
William Wordsworth

The Wild Flower's Song   60
William Blake

The Song of the Flower XXIII   63
Khalil Gibran

The Violet   65
Jane Taylor

The Deserted Garden   66
Elizabeth Barrett Browning

An Old-Fashioned Garden *Ellis Parker Butler*	73
A Red Red Rose *Robert Burns*	75
Flowers in Winter *John Greenleaf Whittier*	76
When Cold December *Dame Edith Louisa Sitwell*	79
That Day You Came *Lizette Woodworth Reese*	83
Editor's Poetry Pick	85
Editor's Flower Pick	89
Editor's Art Pick #1	91
Editor's Art Pick #2	95
Birth Month Flowers	101
State Flowers	103
How You Can Help	107
About Kristen Clark	109

KRISTEN CLARK

FEATURED ARTWORK

Hill Country Blues – Cover by
Renea Menzies

Summertime by   17
Linda MacDonald

Floral Study by Jeremy Pusey   25

Dahlia Aglow by   31
Joy Runscheidt

A Soirée of Sorts by   39
Laurie Smith

Lazy Tulips by Jo Nan Carr   47

Knapweed Metamorphosis by   53
Karey Christensen

Flowers in Flight by   61
Bee Evans

Roses of Remembrance by   71
Karen Nolen

Unimaginable Bouquet by   81
Renea Menzies

KRISTEN CLARK

Shed no tear! O shed no tear!
The flower will bloom another year.
Weep no more! O weep no more!
Young buds sleep in the root's white core.

John Keats, "Faery Songs"

KRISTEN CLARK

A FEW INTRODUCTORY WORDS

Flowers. We paint them. Photograph them. Pick and purchase them. Grow them. Give them. We celebrate them.

The truth is, flowers permeate every part of our lives. They take center stage in our life-changing events, including births, weddings, even funerals, and they grace our homes and gardens with beauty, joy, and peace. It's no wonder they've found their way into the arts. In fact, the painting of flowers has become common place, not only because of their beauty and color, but also because flowers provide the perfect metaphor for the vibrancy of our own lives.

Think of Claude Monet and his painting, Sunflowers, or an untitled painting (Vase of Flowers) by Georgia O'Keeffe. Even Andy Warhol, who struggled much of his life to be taken seriously as an artist, won some acclaim for his piece, Flowers, proof that an artist can't go terribly wrong using flowers as an artistic expression.

This may very well explain why every famous writer has written about flowers or used them as symbols and similes in their work. Writers also understand the deep connection between people and flowers, and use flowers to communicate about life experiences and emotions. Flowers are used to paint pictures in our minds as symbolic references for life, love, and happiness.

And, while flowers are naturally beautiful in and of themselves, it is the artistic arrangement of flowers that further enhances their beauty, giving credence to floral arrangement as an art form. Other popular art forms include paper flowers, clay flowers, dried flowers, not to mention photographs, embroidery, and sculptures.

In fact, flowers and art are intensely intertwined. Just think of the numerous books, songs, and movies named after a flower, demonstrating their role as a source of inspiration.

A few titles that now come to mind include:

- The song, *For the Roses*, by Joni Mitchell
- The book, *Dandelion Wine*, by Ray Bradbury
- The 1958 version of *The Black Orchid*, starring Sophia Loren

Flowers have even fallen victim to some English idioms. You've heard the phrases:

- Coming up roses
- Shrinking violet
- Thorn in your side
- Nip in the bud, and
- Fresh as a daisy

This anthology of poems is drawn from American, British, and French collections, which I hope you find as exhilarating as I do. Nowhere will you read so many creative and elegant descriptions for flowers as you will here, including:

- Fairy gifts
- The fairest blossom
- Censer of our dreams
- A beauteous sisterhood
- Platoons of gold-frocked cavalry

Additionally, I've added photographs of original floral artwork by well-established and award-winning artists to compliment the poetry. My goal, Dear Reader, is to transport you to a world of natural beauty and wonder. This is one of my many passions.

Featuring poems written by Claude McKay, Thomas Carew, Emily Dickson, Robert Frost, and others, this book invites you to explore and discover for yourself the beauty of flowers and their presence in your daily joy.

KRISTEN CLARK

SUMMERTIME
WATERCOLOR, 22X28"
BY LINDA MACDONALD

Linda MacDonald grew up in the North East Scotland. Even at an early age she enjoyed sketching and drawing. After completing her education in small rural Scottish schools she moved to Aberdeen, where she ran her own business and met her husband. After relocating to Houston, Texas in 1997, Linda devoted time to her growing passion for art and its manifestations. She has since studied with various teachers over the years, including Pat Damsgaard, Joy Rumscheidt, Steven Quiller, Betsy Dillard Stroud, and Jann Pollard. Linda is a member of Watercolor Art Society Houston, and Northwest Art League where she won Best Watercolor for a painting of her beloved cat, Suzie. For more information about Linda and her artwork, contact Linda at lindammacdonald@comcast.net.

GOD MADE A LITTLE GENTIAN

EMILY DICKINSON (1830-1886)

God made a little gentian;
It tried to be a rose
And failed, and all the summer laughed.

But just before the snows
There came a purple creature
That ravished all the hill;
And summer hid her forehead,
And mockery was still.

The frosts were her condition;
The Tyrian would not come
Until the North evoked it.

"CREATOR! SHALL I BLOOM?"

EASTER FLOWER

CLAUDE MCKAY (1889-1948)

Far from this foreign Easter damp and chilly
My soul steals to a pear-shaped plot of ground,
Where gleamed the lilac-tinted Easter lily
Soft-scented in the air for yards around;

Alone, without a hint of guardian leaf!
Just like a fragile bell of silver rime,
It burst the tomb for freedom sweet and brief
In the young pregnant year at Eastertime;

And many thought it was a sacred sign,
And some called it the resurrection flower;
And I, a pagan, worshiped at its shrine,
Yielding my heart unto its perfumed power.

THE PRIMROSE

THOMAS CAREW (1595-1640)

Ask me why I send you here
The firstling of the infant year;
Ask me why I send to you
This primrose all bepearled with dew:
I straight will whisper in your ears,
The sweets of love are washed with tears.

Ask me why this flower doth show
So yellow, green, and sickly too;
Ask me why the stalk is weak
And bending, yet it doth not break:
I must tell you, these discover
What doubts and fears are in a lover.

DAISY

FRANCIS THOMPSON (1859-1907)

Where the thistle lifts a purple crown
    Six foot out of the turf,
And the harebell shakes on the windy hill—
    O breath of the distant surf!—

The hills look over on the South,
    And southward dreams the sea;
And with the sea-breeze hand in hand
    Came innocence and she.

Where 'mid the gorse the raspberry
    Red for the gatherer springs;
Two children did we stray and talk
    Wise, idle, childish things.

She listened with big-lipped surprise,
    Breast-deep 'mid flower and spine:
Her skin was like a grape whose veins
    Run snow instead of wine.

She knew not those sweet words she spake,
    Nor knew her own sweet way;
But there's never a bird, so sweet a song
    Thronged in whose throat all day.

Oh, there were flowers in Storrington
   On the turf and on the spray;
But the sweetest flower on Sussex hills
   Was the Daisy-flower that day!

Her beauty smoothed earth's furrowed face.
   She gave me tokens three:—
A look, a word of her winsome mouth,
   And a wild raspberry.

A berry red, a guileless look,
   A still word,—strings of sand!
And yet they made my wild, wild heart
   Fly down to her little hand.

For standing artless as the air,
   And candid as the skies,
She took the berries with her hand,
   And the love with her sweet eyes.

The fairest things have fleetest end,
   Their scent survives their close:
But the rose's scent is bitterness
   To him that loved the rose.

She looked a little wistfully,
   Then went her sunshine way—
The sea's eye had a mist on it,
   And the leaves fell from the day.

She went her unremembering way,
   She went and left in me

The pang of all the partings gone,
    And partings yet to be.

She left me marveling why my soul
    Was sad that she was glad;
At all the sadness in the sweet,
    The sweetness in the sad.

Still, still I seemed to see her, still
    Look up with soft replies,
And take the berries with her hand,
    And the love with her lovely eyes.

Nothing begins, and nothing ends,
    That is not paid with moan,
For we are born in other's pain,
    And perish in our own.

FLORAL STUDY
OIL, 30X40CM
BY JEREMY PUSEY

Jeremy Pusey, born in Bogota, Colombia, works predominantly in the medium of oil, but his talents also include bronze-casting, ceramic, illustration, acting, and teaching. Jeremy completed his BA in Studio Art at UC Santa Cruz. Jeremy says about his art, "There's a perfection, a craftsman-ship, an aesthetic, a beauty which we see in the universe… it's all around us. It's ordered and created and made. When I follow suit in the process of creating in my own life, I'm tapping into that same divine language." Jeremy, his wife Marcy, and their four children currently live in Germany, where Jeremy partners with the Art Factory, Kandern, through weekly open studio painting, art critique, and gallery showings. For more information visit http://www.artpal.com/jeremypusey.

WE SHOULD NOT MIND
SO SMALL A FLOWER

EMILY DICKINSON (1830-1886)

We should not mind so small a flower --
Except it quiet bring
Our little garden that we lost
Back to the Lawn again.

So spicy her Carnations nod –
So drunken, reel her Bees –
So silver steal a hundred flutes
From out a hundred trees –
That whoso sees this little flower
By faith may clear behold
The Bobolinks around the throne
And Dandelions gold.

THE SICK ROSE

WILLIAM BLAKE (1757-1827)

O Rose, thou art sick!
The invisible worm
That flies in the night,
In the howling storm,

Has found out thy bed
Of crimson joy:
And his dark secret love
Does thy life destroy.

THE WILD HONEY-SUCKLE

PHILIP FRENEAU (1752-1832)

Fair flower, that dost so comely grow,
Hid in this silent, dull retreat,
Untouched thy honied blossoms blow,
Unseen thy little branches greet;
No roving foot shall crush thee here,
No busy hand provoke a tear.

By Nature's self in white arrayed,
She bade thee shun the vulgar eye,
And planted here the guardian shade,
And sent soft waters murmuring by;
Thus quietly thy summer goes,
Thy days declining to repose.

Smit with those charms, that must decay,
I grieve to see your future doom;
They died--nor were those flowers more gay,
The flowers that did in Eden bloom;
Unpitying frosts, and Autumn's power
Shall leave no vestige of this flower.

From morning suns and evening dews
At first thy little being came:
If nothing once, you nothing lose,

For when you die you are the same;
The space between, is but an hour,
The frail duration of a flower.

DAHLIA AGLOW
TRANSPARENT WATERCOLOR, 14X10"
BY JOY RUMSCHEIDT

Joy Rumscheidt was born in Montreal and graduated in the Arts from Sir George Williams University, and in Education from McGill University. She is a watercolorist and has been a teacher of watercolor for 38 years in Houston, TX. Joy is a signature member of the Watercolor Art Society of Houston and participates in the Northwest Art League. Joy loves the transparency of watercolor, allowing the layering of washes, which, along with hard and soft edges, creates the beauty of the medium. Please visit Joyrumscheidt.com for more information.

THE TUFT OF FLOWERS

ROBERT FROST (1874-1963)

I went to turn the grass once after one
Who mowed it in the dew before the sun.

The dew was gone that made his blade so keen
Before I came to view the levelled scene.

I looked for him behind an isle of trees;
I listened for his whetstone on the breeze.

But he had gone his way, the grass all mown,
And I must be, as he had been,—alone,

'As all must be,' I said within my heart,
'Whether they work together or apart.'

But as I said it, swift there passed me by
On noiseless wing a bewildered butterfly,

Seeking with memories grown dim overnight
Some resting flower of yesterday's delight.

And once I marked his flight go round and round,
As where some flower lay withering on the ground.

And then he flew as far as eye could see,

And then on tremulous wing came back to me.

I thought of questions that have no reply,
And would have turned to toss the grass to dry;

But he turned first, and led my eye to look
At a tall tuft of flowers beside a brook,

A leaping tongue of bloom the scythe had spared
Beside a reedy brook the scythe had bared.

I left my place to know them by their name,
Finding them butterfly-weed when I came.

The mower in the dew had loved them thus,
By leaving them to flourish, not for us,

Nor yet to draw one thought of ours to him,
But from sheer morning gladness at the brim.

The butterfly and I had lit upon,
Nevertheless, a message from the dawn,

That made me hear the wakening birds around,
And hear his long scythe whispering to the ground,

And feel a spirit kindred to my own;
So that henceforth I worked no more alone;

But glad with him, I worked as with his aid,
And weary, sought at noon with him the shade;

And dreaming, as it were, held brotherly speech
With one whose thought I had not hoped to reach.

'Men work together,' I told him from the heart,
'Whether they work together or apart.'

THE GODDESS IN THE WOOD

RUPERT BROOKE (1887-1915)

In a flowered dell the Lady Venus stood,
   Amazed with sorrow. Down the morning one
   Far golden horn in the gold of trees and sun
Rang out; and held; and died. . . . She thought the wood
Grew quieter. Wing, and leaf, and pool of light
   Forgot to dance. Dumb lay the unfalling stream;
   Life one eternal instant rose in dream
Clear out of time, poised on a golden height. . . .

Till a swift terror broke the abrupt hour.
The gold waves purled amidst the green above her;
   And a bird sang. With one sharp-taken breath,
By sunlit branches and unshaken flower,
The immortal limbs flashed to the human lover,
   And the immortal eyes to look on death.

THE BLUEBELL

ANNE BRONTE (1820-1849)

A fine and subtle spirit dwells
In every little flower,
Each one its own sweet feeling breathes
With more or less of power.

There is a silent eloquence
In every wild bluebell
That fills my softened heart with bliss
That words could never tell.

Yet I recall not long ago
A bright and sunny day,
'Twas when I led a toilsome life
So many leagues away;

That day along a sunny road
All carelessly I strayed,
Between two banks where smiling flowers
Their varied hues displayed.

Before me rose a lofty hill,
Behind me lay the sea,
My heart was not so heavy then
As it was wont to be.

Less harassed than at other times
I saw the scene was fair,

And spoke and laughed to those around,
As if I knew no care.

But when I looked upon the bank
My wandering glances fell
Upon a little trembling flower,
A single sweet bluebell.

Whence came that rising in my throat,
That dimness in my eye?
Why did those burning drops distil --
Those bitter feelings rise?

O, that lone flower recalled to me
My happy childhood's hours
When bluebells seemed like fairy gifts
A prize among the flowers,

Those sunny days of merriment
When heart and soul were free,
And when I dwelt with kindred hearts
That loved and cared for me.

I had not then mid heartless crowds
To spend a thankless life
In seeking after others' weal
With anxious toil and strife.

'Sad wanderer, weep those blissful times
That never may return!'
The lovely floweret seemed to say,
And thus it made me mourn.

A SOIREE OF SORTS
ACRYLIC, 5X7"
BY LAURIE SMITH

Laurie Smith is a happily married wife, mother of two amazing daughters, Mimi to her grandbabies, Christian woman, and entrepreneur of the Etsy online shop, Willow Creek Sparrow, where she sells everything vintage along with her own hand crafted treasures. In her spare time, she loves perusing bookstores, hunting down out of the way antique shops, trying to grow roses without much luck, and she is a freelance photographer. One thing she loves most is a good pencil. Please visit Laurie at https://www.etsy.com/shop/WillowCreekSparrow.

THE ROSE

WILLIAM BROWNE (1590-1645)

A ROSE, as fair as ever saw the North,
Grew in a little garden all alone;
A sweeter flower did Nature ne'er put forth,
Nor fairer garden yet was never known:
The maidens danced about it morn and noon,
And learned bards of it their ditties made;
The nimble fairies by the pale-faced moon
Water'd the root and kiss'd her pretty shade.

But well-a-day!--the gardener careless grew;
The maids and fairies both were kept away,
And in a drought the caterpillars threw
Themselves upon the bud and every spray.

God shield the stock! If heaven send no supplies,
The fairest blossom of the garden dies.

LITANIES OF THE ROSE

REMY DE GOURMONT (1858-1915)

Rose with dark eyes,
mirror of your nothingness,
rose with dark eyes,
make us believe in the mystery,
hypocrite flower,
flower of silence.

Rose the color of pure gold,
oh safe deposit of the ideal,
rose the color of pure gold,
give us the key of your womb,
hypocrite flower,
flower of silence.

Rose the color of silver,
censer of our dreams,
rose the color of silver,
take our heart and turn it into smoke,
hypocrite flower,
flower of silence.

THE DEATH OF THE FLOWERS

WILLIAM CULLEN BRYANT (1794-1878)

THE MELANCHOLY days have come the saddest of the year
Of wailing winds and naked woods and meadows brown and sere;
Heaped in the hollows of the grove the autumn leaves lie dead;
They rustle to the eddying gust and to the rabbit's tread;
The robin and the wren are flown and from the shrubs the jay
And from the wood-top calls the crow through all the gloomy day.

Where are the flowers the fair young flowers that lately sprang and stood
In brighter light and softer airs a beauteous sisterhood?
Alas! they all are in their graves the gentle race of flowers
Are lying in their lowly beds with the fair and good of ours.
The rain is falling where they lie but the cold November rain
Calls not from out the gloomy earth the lovely ones again.

The wind-flower and the violet they perished long ago
And the brier-rose and the orchid died amid the summer glow;

But on the hill the goldenrod and the aster in the wood
And the blue sunflower by the brook in autumn beauty stood
Till fell the frost from the clear cold heaven as falls the plague on men
And the brightness of their smile was gone from upland glade and glen.

And now when comes the calm mild day as still such days will come
To call the squirrel and the bee from out their winter home;
When the sound of dropping nuts is heard though all the trees are still
And twinkle in the smoky light the waters of the rill
The south wind searches for the flowers whose fragrance late he bore
And sighs to find them in the wood and by the stream no more.

And then I think of one who in her youthful beauty died
The fair meek blossom that grew up and faded by my side.

In the cold moist earth we laid her when the forests cast the leaf
And we wept that one so lovely should have a life so brief:
Yet not unmeet it was that one like that young friend of ours
So gentle and so beautiful should perish with the flowers.

Fair flowers are not left
standing along the wayside long.

German Proverb

THE FLOWER MUST NOT BLAME THE BEE

EMILY DICKINSON (1830-1886)

The Flower must not blame the Bee --
That seeketh his felicity
Too often at her door --

But teach the Footman from Vevay --
Mistress is "not at home" -- to say --
To people -- anymore!

LAZY TULIPS
OIL ON CANVASS, 16X20"
BY JO NAN CARR

Jo Nan Carr started art lessons when tole painting was the rage in the 60s. Afterward, she found several art teachers who specialized in oil painting processes, from copying old masters to still life and other realistic subjects. About ten years ago her painting world exploded with energy and freedom when she found acrylic workshops for mixed media, experimental and collage.

FANCY

JOHN KEATS (1795–1821)

Ever let the Fancy roam,
Pleasure never is at home:
At a touch sweet Pleasure melteth,
Like to bubbles when rain pelteth;
Then let winged Fancy wander
Through the thought still spread beyond her:
Open wide the mind's cage-door,
She'll dart forth, and cloudward soar.
O sweet Fancy! let her loose;
Summer's joys are spoilt by use,
And the enjoying of the Spring
Fades as does its blossoming;
Autumn's red-lipp'd fruitage too,
Blushing through the mist and dew,
Cloys with tasting: What do then?
Sit thee by the ingle, when
The sear faggot blazes bright,
Spirit of a winter's night;
When the soundless earth is muffled,
And the caked snow is shuffled
From the ploughboy's heavy shoon;
When the Night doth meet the Noon
In a dark conspiracy
To banish Even from her sky.
Sit thee there, and send abroad,
With a mind self-overaw'd,

Fancy, high-commission'd:—send her!
She has vassals to attend her:
She will bring, in spite of frost,
Beauties that the earth hath lost;
She will bring thee, all together,
All delights of summer weather;
All the buds and bells of May,
From dewy sward or thorny spray;
All the heaped Autumn's wealth,
With a still, mysterious stealth:
She will mix these pleasures up
Like three fit wines in a cup,
And thou shalt quaff it:—thou shalt hear
Distant harvest-carols clear;
Rustle of the reaped corn;
Sweet birds antheming the morn:
And, in the same moment, hark!
'Tis the early April lark,
Or the rooks, with busy caw,
Foraging for sticks and straw.
Thou shalt, at one glance, behold
The daisy and the marigold;
White-plum'd lillies, and the first
Hedge-grown primrose that hath burst;
Shaded hyacinth, always
Sapphire queen of the mid-May;
And every leaf, and every flower
Pearled with the self-same shower.
Thou shalt see the field-mouse peep
Meagre from its celled sleep;
And the snake all winter-thin
Cast on sunny bank its skin;

Freckled nest-eggs thou shalt see
Hatching in the hawthorn-tree,
When the hen-bird's wing doth rest
Quiet on her mossy nest;
Then the hurry and alarm
When the bee-hive casts its swarm;
Acorns ripe down-pattering,
While the autumn breezes sing.

Oh, sweet Fancy! let her loose;
Everything is spoilt by use:
Where's the cheek that doth not fade,
Too much gaz'd at? Where's the maid
Whose lip mature is ever new?
Where's the eye, however blue,
Doth not weary? Where's the face
One would meet in every place?
Where's the voice, however soft,
One would hear so very oft?
At a touch sweet Pleasure melteth
Like to bubbles when rain pelteth.
Let, then, winged Fancy find
Thee a mistress to thy mind:
Dulcet-ey'd as Ceres' daughter,
Ere the God of Torment taught her
How to frown and how to chide;
With a waist and with a side
White as Hebe's, when her zone
Slipt its golden clasp, and down
Fell her kirtle to her feet,
While she held the goblet sweet

And Jove grew languid.—Break the mesh
Of the Fancy's silken leash;
Quickly break her prison-string
And such joys as these she'll bring.—
Let the winged Fancy roam,
Pleasure never is at home.

KNAPWEED METAMORPHOSIS
COLORED PENCILS DIGITALLY ALTERED
IN WATERCOLOR SPONGE
BY KAREY CHRISTENSEN

Karey Christensen, born and raised mostly in the Inland Northwest, has been an artist since conception. Taught to love drawing from her Grandmother. Taught to love good food and drink from her brother. Taught to love life and laugh by her daughter. Taught to appreciate the love of a good man. Taught to love photography from her mom. And taught that forgiving, loving, and losing someone close to you, while making us miss them almost more than living, makes us who we are and appreciate living even more.

A TULIP GARDEN

AMY LOWELL (1874–1925)

Guarded within the old red wall's embrace,
Marshalled like soldiers in gay company,
The tulips stand arrayed. Here infantry
Wheels out into the sunlight. What bold grace
Sets off their tunics, white with crimson lace!
Here are platoons of gold-frocked cavalry,
With scarlet sabres tossing in the eye
Of purple batteries, every gun in place.
Forward they come, with flaunting colors spread,
With torches burning, stepping out in time
To some quick, unheard march. Our ears are dead,
We cannot catch the tune. In pantomime
Parades that army. With our utmost powers
We hear the wind stream through a bed of flowers.

ASKING FOR ROSES

ROBERT FROST (1874–1963)

A house that lacks, seemingly, mistress and master,
With doors that none but the wind ever closes,
Its floor all littered with glass and with plaster;
It stands in a garden of old-fashioned roses.

I pass by that way in the gloaming with Mary;
'I wonder,' I say, 'who the owner of those is.'
'Oh, no one you know,' she answers me airy,
'But one we must ask if we want any roses.'

So we must join hands in the dew coming coldly
There in the hush of the wood that reposes,
And turn and go up to the open door boldly,
And knock to the echoes as beggars for roses.

'Pray, are you within there, Mistress Who-were-you?'
'Tis Mary that speaks and our errand discloses.
'Pray, are you within there? Bestir you, bestir you!
'Tis summer again; there's two come for roses.

'A word with you, that of the singer recalling--
Old Herrick: a saying that every maid knows is
A flower unplucked is but left to the falling,
And nothing is gained by not gathering roses.'

We do not loosen our hands' intertwining
(Not caring so very much what she supposes),
There when she comes on us mistily shining
And grants us by silence the boon of her roses.

TO THE SAME FLOWER
(SECOND POEM)

WILLIAM WORDSWORTH (1770–1850)

With little here to do or see
Of things that in the great world be,
Daisy! again I talk to thee,
For thou art worthy,
Thou unassuming Common-place
Of Nature, with that homely face,
And yet with something of a grace,
Which Love makes for thee!

Oft on the dappled turf at ease
I sit, and play with similes,
Loose types of things through all degrees,
Thoughts of thy raising:
And many a fond and idle name
I give to thee, for praise or blame,
As is the humor of the game,
While I am gazing.

A nun demure of lowly port;
Or sprightly maiden, of Love's court,
In thy simplicity the sport
Of all temptations;
A queen in crown of rubies drest;
A starveling in a scanty vest;
Are all, as seems to suit thee best,
Thy appellations.

A little cyclops, with one eye
Staring to threaten and defy,
That thought comes next--and instantly
The freak is over,
The shape will vanish--and behold
A silver shield with boss of gold,
That spreads itself, some faery bold
In fight to cover!

I see thee glittering from afar--
And then thou art a pretty star;
Not quite so fair as many are
In heaven above thee!
Yet like a star, with glittering crest,
Self-poised in air thou seem'st to rest;--
May peace come never to his nest,
Who shall reprove thee!

Bright 'Flower'! for by that name at last,
When all my reveries are past,
I call thee, and to that cleave fast,
Sweet silent creature!
That breath'st with me in sun and air,
Do thou, as thou art wont, repair
My heart with gladness, and a share
Of thy meek nature!

THE WILD FLOWER'S SONG

WILLIAM BLAKE (1757-1827)

As I wander'd the forest,
The green leaves among,
I heard a wild flower
Singing a song.

I slept in the Earth
In the silent night,
I murmur'd my fears
And I felt delight.

In the morning I went
As rosy as morn,
To seek for new joy;
But O! met with scorn.

FLOWERS IN FLIGHT
PRISMACOLOR COLORED PENCILS, 6X8"
BY BEE EVANS

Avonechay B. Evans, better known as Bee, was born in Thailand in 1979. Her move to the U.S. began in early childhood much like her artistic process.

Still life colored pencil drawings, vivid watercolor paintings, and mixed media pieces are found throughout the Evans collection. Her work is characterized by vibrant colors, intricate shapes, and flowing compositions. Beneath and beyond her art lies universal themes of creation, life, love and transformation. Her illustrations incorporate the beauty of nature while offering symbolic meanings to discover and explore.

Bee was awarded Best of Show, among 25,000 entries, in the 1997 Houston Livestock Show and Rodeo Art contest. Ms. Evans studied at the nationally acclaimed Advanced Visual Arts program with Carver H.S. She is a member of the Northwest Art League and currently lives and works in Houston, TX.

Feel free to contact Bee at https://www.facebook.com/TheBuzzOnBee or TheBuzzOnBee@Outlook.com.

THE SONG OF THE FLOWER XXIII

KHALIL GIBRAN (1883–1931)

I am a kind word uttered and repeated
By the voice of Nature;
I am a star fallen from the
Blue tent upon the green carpet.
I am the daughter of the elements
With whom Winter conceived;
To whom Spring gave birth; I was
Reared in the lap of Summer and I
Slept in the bed of Autumn.

At dawn I unite with the breeze
To announce the coming of light;
At eventide I join the birds
In bidding the light farewell.

The plains are decorated with
My beautiful colors, and the air
Is scented with my fragrance.

As I embrace Slumber the eyes of
Night watch over me, and as I
Awaken I stare at the sun, which is
The only eye of the day.

I drink dew for wine, and hearken to
The voices of the birds, and dance

To the rhythmic swaying of the grass.

I am the lover's gift; I am the wedding wreath;
I am the memory of a moment of happiness;
I am the last gift of the living to the dead;
I am a part of joy and a part of sorrow.

But I look up high to see only the light,
And never look down to see my shadow.
This is wisdom which man must learn.

THE VIOLET

JANE TAYLOR (1783–1824)

Down in a green and shady bed,
A modest violet grew;
Its stalk was bent, it hung its head
As if to hide from view.
And yet it was a lovely flower,
Its color bright and fair;
It might have graced a rosy bower,
Instead of hiding there.

Yet thus it was content to bloom,
In modest tints arrayed;
And there diffused a sweet perfume,
Within the silent shade.

Then let me to the valley go
This pretty flower to see;
That I may also learn to grow
In sweet humility.

THE DESERTED GARDEN

ELIZABETH BARRETT BROWNING
(1806–1861)

I MIND me in the days departed,
How often underneath the sun
With childish bounds I used to run
To a garden long deserted.

The beds and walks were vanish'd quite;
And wheresoe'er had struck the spade,
The greenest grasses Nature laid,
To sanctify her right.

I call'd the place my wilderness,
For no one enter'd there but I.
The sheep look'd in, the grass to espy,
And pass'd it ne'ertheless.

The trees were interwoven wild,
And spread their boughs enough about
To keep both sheep and shepherd out,
But not a happy child.

Adventurous joy it was for me!
I crept beneath the boughs, and found
A circle smooth of mossy ground
Beneath a poplar-tree.

Old garden rose-trees hedged it in,
Bedropt with roses waxen-white,
Well satisfied with dew and light,
And careless to be seen.

Long years ago, it might befall,
When all the garden flowers were trim,
The grave old gardener prided him
On these the most of all.

Some Lady, stately overmuch,
Here moving with a silken noise,
Has blush'd beside them at the voice
That liken'd her to such.

Or these, to make a diadem,
She often may have pluck'd and twined;
Half-smiling as it came to mind,
That few would look at them.

O, little thought that Lady proud,
A child would watch her fair white rose,
When buried lay her whiter brows,
And silk was changed for shroud!

Nor thought that gardener (full of scorns
For men unlearn'd and simple phrase)
A child would bring it all its praise,
By creeping through the thorns!

To me upon my low moss seat,
Though never a dream the roses sent

Of science or love's compliment,
I ween they smelt as sweet.

It did not move my grief to see
The trace of human step departed:
Because the garden was deserted,
The blither place for me!

Friends, blame me not! a narrow ken
Hath childhood 'twixt the sun and sward:
We draw the moral afterward
We feel the gladness then.

And gladdest hours for me did glide
In silence at the rose-tree wall:
A thrush made gladness musical
Upon the other side.

Nor he nor I did e'er incline
To peck or pluck the blossoms white:
How should I know but that they might
Lead lives as glad as mine?

To make my hermit-home complete,
I brought clear water from the spring
Praised in its own low murmuring,
And cresses glossy wet.

And so, I thought, my likeness grew
(Without the melancholy tale)
To 'gentle hermit of the dale,'
And Angelina too.

For oft I read within my nook
Such minstrel stories; till the breeze
Made sounds poetic in the trees,
And then I shut the book.

If I shut this wherein I write,
I hear no more the wind athwart
Those trees, nor feel that childish heart
Delighting in delight.

My childhood from my life is parted,
My footstep from the moss which drew
Its fairy circle round: anew
The garden is deserted.

Another thrush may there rehearse
The madrigals which sweetest are;
No more for me! myself afar
Do sing a sadder verse.

Ah me! ah me! when erst I lay
In that child's-nest so greenly wrought,
I laugh'd unto myself and thought,
'The time will pass away.

And still I laugh'd, and did not fear
But that, whene'er was pass'd away
The childish time, some happier play
My womanhood would cheer.

I knew the time would pass away;
And yet, beside the rose-tree wall,

Dear God, how seldom, if at all,
Did I look up to pray!

The time is past: and now that grows
The cypress high among the trees,
And I behold white sepulchers
As well as the white rose,

When wiser, meeker thoughts are given,
And I have learnt to lift my face,
Reminded how earth's greenest place
The color draws from heaven,

It something saith for earthly pain,
But more for heavenly promise free,
That I who was, would shrink to be
That happy child again.

FLOWERS: The Language of Artists & Poets

ROSES OF REMEMBRANCE
EMROIDERY, 10 X 17.5"
BY KAREN NOLEN

Karen Nolen enjoys the variety of flowers our Creator has made. She uses several artistic mediums to show her love of flowers— from cross-stitch and embroidery to photographs and creating photo books. Her love is being outdoors and taking photos of flowers. She currently lives in the greater Phoenix metropolitan area, and is employed as a paralegal. She has 3 sons, 2 daughters-in-law and 5 grandchildren.

AN OLD-FASHIONED GARDEN

ELLIS PARKER BUTLER (1869-1937)

Strange, is it not? She was making her garden,
 Planting the old-fashioned flowers that day—
Bleeding-hearts tender and bachelors-buttons—
 Spreading the seeds in the old-fashioned way.

Just in the old fashioned way, too, our quarrel
 Grew until, angrily, she set me free—
Planting, indeed, bleeding hearts for the two of us,—
 Ordaining bachelor's buttons for me.

Envoi

Strange, was it not? But seeds planted in anger
 Sour in the earth and, ere long, a decay
Withered the bleeding hearts, blighted the buttons,
 And—we were wed—in the old-fashioned way.

Flowers are the sweetest things God ever made, and forgot to put a soul into.

Henry Beecher, *Life Thoughts*, 1858

A RED RED ROSE

ROBERT BURNS (1759-1796)

O, my Luve's like a red, red rose,
That's newly sprung in June.

O, my Luve's like a melody
That's sweetly play'd in tune.

As fair as thou, my bonnie lass,
So deep in luve am I;
And I will love thee still, my dear,
Till a' the seas gang dry.

Till a' the seas gang dry, my dear,
And the rocks melt wi' the sun:
I will love thee till, my dear,
While the sands o' life shall run:

And fare thee well, my only luve!
And fare thee well, a while!
And I will come again, my luve,
Tho' it were ten thousand mile.

FLOWERS IN WINTER

JOHN GREENLEAF WHITTIER
(1807-1892)

How strange to greet, this frosty morn,
In graceful counterfeit of flower,
These children of the meadows, born
Of sunshine and of showers!

How well the conscious wood retains
The pictures of its flower-sown home,
The lights and shades, the purple stains,
And golden hues of bloom!

It was a happy thought to bring
To the dark season's frost and rime
This painted memory of spring,
This dream of summertime.

Our hearts are lighter for its sake,
Our fancy's age renews its youth,
And dim-remembered fictions take
The guise of present truth.

A wizard of the Merrimac, -
So old ancestral legends say, -
Could call green leaf and blossom back
To frosted stem and spray.

The dry logs of the cottage wall,
Beneath his touch, put out their leaves;
The clay-bound swallow, at his call,
Played round the icy eaves.

The settler saw his oaken flail
Take bud, and bloom before his eyes;
From frozen pools he saw the pale
Sweet summer lilies rise.

To their old homes, by man profaned
Came the sad dryads, exiled long,
And through their leafy tongues complained
Of household use and wrong.

The beechen platter sprouted wild,
The pipkin wore its old-time green,
The cradle o'er the sleeping child
Became a leafy screen.

Haply our gentle friend hath met,
While wandering in her sylvan quest,
Haunting his native woodlands yet,
That Druid of the West;

And while the dew on leaf and flower
Glistened in the moonlight clear and still,
Learned the dusk wizard's spell of power,
And caught his trick of skill.

But welcome, be it new or old,
The gift which makes the day more bright,
And paints, upon the ground of cold
And darkness, warmth and light!

Without is neither gold nor green;
Within, for birds, the birch-logs sing;
Yet, summer-like, we sit between
The autumn and the spring.

The one, with bridal blush of rose,
And sweetest breath of woodland balm,
And one whose matron lips unclose
In smiles of saintly calm.

Fill soft and deep, O winter snow!
The sweet azalea's oaken dells,
And hide the banks where roses blow
And swing the azure bells!

O'erlay the amber violet's leaves,
The purple aster's brookside home,
Guard all the flowers her pencil gives
A live beyond their bloom.

And she, when spring comes round again,
By greening slope and singing flood
Shall wander, seeking, not in vain
Her darlings of the wood.

WHEN COLD DECEMBER

DAME EDITH LOUISA SITWELL
(1887-1964)

WHEN cold December
Froze to grisamber
The jangling bells on the sweet rose-trees--
Then fading slow
And furred is the snow
As the almond's sweet husk--
And smelling like musk.

The snow amygdaline
Under the eglantine
Where the bristling stars shine
Like a gilt porcupine--
The snow confesses
The little Princesses
On their small chioppines
Dance under the orpines.

See the casuistries
Of their slant fluttering eyes--
Gilt as the zodiac
(Dancing Herodiac).

Only the snow slides
Like gilded myrrh--
From the rose-branches--hides
Rose-roots that stir.

UNIMAGINABLE BOUQUET
OIL ON CANVAS, 14X11"
BY RENEA MENZIES

Renea Menzies' abstract art has bold influences that are inspired by many facets of her individualism. While she is a native Texan, she has traveled the globe to some of the most exotic locations in the world. Her sense of style is heavily influenced by the many cultures she has had a chance to experience. Additionally, her sculpted oil paintings display the intricate marriage of technique and color, bringing her work to life and inspiring movement of the imagination in a textured oasis. For more information, visit www.reneamenzies.com.

THAT DAY YOU CAME

LIZETTE WOODWORTH REESE
(1856-1935)

Such special sweetness was about
 That day God sent you here,
I knew the lavender was out,
 And it was mid of year.

Their common way the great winds blew,
 The ships sailed out to sea;
Yet ere that day was spent I knew
 Mine own had come to me.

As after song some snatch of tune
 Lurks still in grass or bough,
So, somewhat of the end o' June
 Lurks in each weather now.

The young year sets the buds astir,
 The old year strips the trees;
But ever in my lavender
 I hear the brawling bees.

For me the jasmine buds unfold
 And silver daisies star the lea,
The crocus hoards the sunset gold,
 And the wild rose breathes for me.

I feel the sap through the bough returning,
 I share the skylark's transport fine,
I know the fountain's wayward yearning,
 I love, and the world is mine!

I love, and thoughts that sometime grieved,
 Still well remembered, grieve not me;
From all that darkened and deceived
 Upsoars my spirit free.

For soft the hours repeat one story,
 Sings the sea one strain divine;
My clouds arise all flushed with glory --
 I love, and the world is mine!

EDITOR'S POETRY PICK

Before I name my favorite pick of poems, it's important for you to understand what I look for in poetry and prose:

> I like poems that are simple and easy to read.
>
> I like words that rhyme.
>
> I like verses that dance on a melody and easily roll off the tongue.
>
> I like stories that swim in colorful imagery.
>
> I like the whimsical and capricious.

That's why my pick is "The Song of the Flower XXIII" by Khalil Gibran (pg 63).

Khalil Gibran was a Lebanese American artist, poet, and writer. Born in the town of Bsharri, known today as Lebanon, he emigrated with his family as a young man to the United States, where he studied art and began his career in literature.

Gibran is mostly known for his 1923 book, *The Prophet*, an early example of inspirational fiction, including a series of philosophical essays written in poetic English prose. The book sold well despite a cool critical reception and became extremely popular in the 1960s counterculture. Gibran is considered the third best-selling poet of all time, behind Shakespeare and Lao-Tzu.

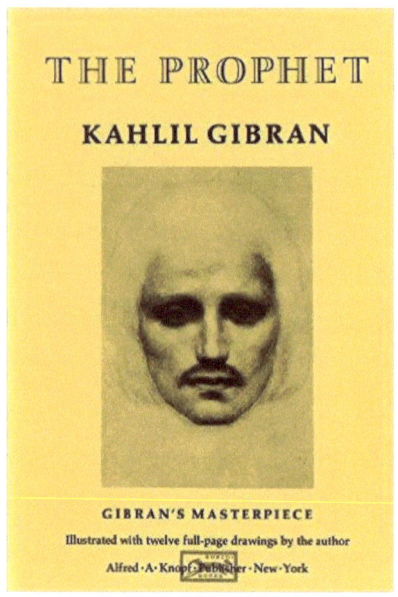

Book available on Amazon.

What I love about his poem, "The Song of the Flower XXIII", is that it is written from the perspective of the flower, meaning the flower is speaking the words in the poem. I envision a single flower in the middle of an expansive field of many, telling me about herself, life with her thousands of brothers and sisters, and days spent reaching toward the warmth of the sunlight.

This poem initially brought to mind images of summer-long perennials, created just for their show of color against a green backdrop of grassy hues. I thought of sun-loving flowers in an open area, enriched with good fertile soil and soft gentle breezes. In particular, I thought of bellflowers, coneflowers, coreopsis, and blanket flowers.

Reading further, I thought of lilies and envisioned a vast field of white and yellow lilies, swaying in a soft wind and twinkling like stars against a green sky. I imagined them celebrating their role as children of the Spring, dancing in the breeze and announcing the light of each new and radiant day. I could even smell their collective fragrance in the air.

The references at the end of the poem, signifying various moments of celebration and sorrow – such as love, weddings, and funerals - reminded me of white stargazers.

The last lines in particular remind me of the human condition and heart of man, and my personal desire to continuously look up – toward the comfort of my Heavenly Father – and never down toward the despair found in the dark of the shadows of Life. Words that came to mind included: gratitude, blessings, and awe.

> *Forget not that the earth delights to feel your bare feet and the winds long to play with your hair.*
>
> *~Kahlil Gibran*

Now I ask you: in what way does this poem move you?

EDITORS FLOWER PICK

Choosing a favorite flower was a little easier than choosing a favorite poem, or art piece for that matter. I like simple. I like clean lines. I like the use of white space, and I like elements that compliment other elements easily. I also like the idea of "low maintenance," especially in the hectic and sometimes overwhelming schedules of our current times. That why my flower pick is the daisy.

I also like daisies because they spread and grow easily. Some areas qualify them as fast-growing weeds, and I'm okay with weeds as long as they are pretty. Daisies are pretty.

My husband likes Daisies because their leaves are edible and can be used in salads. He knows that daisy leaves are closely related to artichokes and are high in Vitamin C. Yes, he's the Mountain Man Gourmet in our family and we eat like kings at our house. ☺

But mostly, I love their familiar white petals and yellow centers. I love their smooth and leafless stems and long slender stalks. I love how daisies are plentiful and never a rarity, except for in Antarctica.

And I love how easily they show off or compliment other flowers in an arrangement. They are the perfect friend, always letting their colleagues and peers show-off and bask in the spotlight.

And yet, they each have their own unequalled beauty and can enhance any vase, either as a single flower or as a large bunch tied together with a simple twine or cord.

Finally, I love how daisies represent and symbolize purity and innocence. No wonder children have used them over the centuries to make "daisy chains".

And, while I don't love bees, bees love daisies too, making daisies an important friend to the honey-making process. Honey I do like!

Now I ask you, Dear Reader, which flower is your personal favorite?

EDITOR'S ART PICK #1

Choosing a favorite piece of artwork from those provided in this collection was extremely difficult. As a mixed-media artist myself, I found the talent presented here in terms of skill and interpretation not only impressive, but also a little intimidating. Kudos to every artist featured in this book. Well done!

I chose two favorites, the first of which is Hill Country Blues, Oil on Canvas, featured on the cover of this book, painted by Renea Menzies.

When I first saw this piece, I was absolutely stunned. It was so vastly different from the many pieces I've seen over the years, not only in terms of vibrancy but also in originality. Many artworks feature thick broad strokes, but none that appear so divinely free and natural.

Please meet, Renea Menzies, the artist. Art enthusiasts say her use of oils creates a thick buttery appearance, similar to ribbon candy. I couldn't agree more.

Using a pallet knife, she blends a variety of colors to move the paint around the canvas, creating a dimensional appearance in her shapes and contours. Upon looking at this particular piece, I was left with a marked and lasting impression, not to mention a slight craving for sugary hard candy.

I featured this piece, Hill Country Blues, as the cover artwork because this piece held my breath captive. I could sense immediately the artist's deep connection with nature.

Just look at how the distinctive form and movement of each petal and leaf are brilliantly captured. The strokes are luminescent and revealing of life's every glint and shadow. And the blues and greens in this piece are mesmerizing and sing of soothing ocean waves. I can almost feel the cool breeze carrying the scent of fresh air, rain, and a face full of clean dry towels.

I knew immediately this work was sculpted from an artist who understands the deep connection between flowers and people, between life experiences and emotions, and the symbolic reference for life, love, and happiness.

Renea Menzies works exclusively with oil and has developed an original and popular floral style that has landed her work in prestigious galleries across the country. Additionally, her work has inspired The Renea Collection of products, including her umbrella and scarf collection, both of which are now on my Christmas list!

KRISTEN CLARK

EDITOR'S ART PICK #2

Ever since I was a little girl, I have been drawn to the art of the needle and thread. The precision and patience embodied in a regal piece of embroidery is to be admired and held in high regard. To this day, I treasure my Grandmother's hand-stitched runners with which I adorn my dining room table. That's why my second choice of artwork is Roses of Remembrance by Karen Nolen, featured on page 71.

The subtle shades and attention to detail in this piece are marvelous and inspire images of myself sitting in a heavily adorned parlor, surrounded by velvet curtains and burgundy upholstered furniture while admiring this particular floral arrangement, eyeing its dropped leaves and petals. I can even almost smell the scent of old fashioned roses and the dirt from which they sprung. Yes, this is one of my favorite works of art.

Embroidery as an art form is not only admirable, it is also historical. In fact, the earliest samples of handmade embroidery were discovered in ancient Egypt, Persia, China, India, Russia and England, with each country portraying its unique style in terms of design, cultural embellishment, history, and traditions. In fact, Embroidery has been dated to the Warring States period (5th-3rd century BC) of ancient China.

When I think of embroidery, I am reminded of the Victorian era and the elaborate freehand stitching of that time. In fact, *The Language of Flowers*, a dictionary of symbolic meanings assigned to individual flowers, was established in Europe during the early 19th century as a result of the leisure classes' interests in botany and a social preoccupation with romance and chivalry.

Embroidery, closely linked to the Victorians' definition of femininity, could have been an ideal form through which women expressed what otherwise could not be said. The prolific amount of publications on the Language of Flowers and the popularity of flowers as a subject in embroidery designs throughout the Victorian era suggest the possibility that flower symbolism was used in floral embroidery as a method through which women could silently express themselves.

In a report called, "Silent Needles, Speaking Flowers: The Language of Flowers as a Tool for Communication in Women's Embroidery in Victorian Britain", published by Mary Brooks and Christen Elaine Ericsson through the University of Nebraska in Lincoln, it is noted,

> Beginning in the 18th century, rumors spread across Europe of a secret flower language being practiced in Turkey. This is largely a result of the letters of Lady Mary Wortley Montagu, who, while writing home to England from the Turkish Embassy, discussed "a mysterious language of love and gallantry". In a letter to a friend, she described the use of objects to communicate, calling it a "Turkish love letter".
>
> She wrote of this language: "There is no color, no flower, no weed, no fruit, herb, pebble, or feather that has not a verse belonging to it: and you may quarrel, reproach, or send letters of passion, friendship, or civility, or even of news, without ever inking your fingers". Over the course of the century, the rumors became interest, and then practice. Until, by the early 19th century, the development of a formalized Language of Flowers had occurred. This took the form of a dictionary of symbolic meanings assigned to individual flowers, which thus became

generally known to society as a method of silent communication.

I am mesmerized by the possibility of a language using flowers as a form of communication in embroidery, and I wonder what I might have wanted to say during such times.

I am also mesmerized by the story of embroidery as outlined in the Project Gutenberg eBook of The Development of Embroidery in America, by Candace Wheeler, which explains,

> The story of embroidery includes in its history all the work of the needle since Eve sewed fig leaves together in the Garden of Eden. We are the inheritors of the knowledge and skill of all the daughters of Eve in all that concerns its use since the beginning of time.

And while I'm not a feminist at heart, this particular notation embodies a universal sense of connectedness for women everywhere. We really do share a love of flowers as a symbol for our connection to each other.

Long live the embroidered flower!

FLOWERS: The Language of Artists & Poets

I will be the gladdest thing
Under the sun!
I will touch a hundred flowers
And not pick one.

Edna St. Vincent Millay
"Afternoon on a Hill"

BIRTH MONTH FLOWERS

Month	Flower
January	Carnation
February	Iris, Violet
March	Daffodil
April	Daisy, Peonies
May	Lily, Lily of the Valley
June	Rose
July	Delphinium
August	Dahlia, Gladiolus
September	Aster, Forget-me-not
October	Calendula (aka Marigold)
November	Chrysanthemum
December	Poinsettia, Holly, Narcissus

KRISTEN CLARK

STATE FLOWERS

Alabama	Camellia
Alaska	Forget-me-not
Arizona	Saguaro Cactus blossom
Arkansas	Apple blossom
California	California Poppy
Colorado	Rocky Mountain Columbine
Connecticut	Mountain laurel
Delaware	Peach blossom
Florida	Orange blossom
Georgia	Cherokee Rose
Hawaii	Hawaiian hibiscus
Idaho	Mock Orange
Illinois	Purple Violet
Indiana	Peony
Iowa	Wild Prairie Rose
Kansas	Sunflower
Kentucky	Goldenrod
Louisiana	Magnolia
Maine	White pine cone and tassel
Maryland	Black-eyed susan

Massachusetts	Mayflower
Michigan	Apple blossom
Minnesota	Pink and white lady's slipper
Mississippi	Magnolia
Missouri	Hawthorn
Montana	Bitterroot
Nebraska	Goldenrod
Nevada	Sagebrush
New Hampshire	Purple lilac
New Jersey	Violet
New Mexico	Yucca flower
New York	Rose
North Carolina	American Dogwood
North Dakota	Wild Prairie Rose
Ohio	Scarlet Carnation
Oklahoma	Oklahoma Rose
Oregon	Oregon grape
Pennsylvania	Mountain Laurel
Rhode Island	Violet
South Carolina	Yellow Jessamine
South Dakota	Pasque flower
Tennessee	Iris
Texas	Bluebonnet

Utah	Sego lily
Vermont	Red Clover
Virginia	American Dogwood
Washington	Coast Rhododendron
West Virginia	Rhododendron
Wisconsin	Wood Violet
Wyoming	Indian Paintbrush

KRISTEN CLARK

HOW YOU CAN HELP

Did you enjoy this book? Please help spread the word!

One great way is to post a comment about it on Facebook and other social media forums, inviting your friends to have a look. Here's a simple message you can use:

> Just finished reading this book, *Flowers: The Language of Artists & Poets,* and I can't tell you how inspiring it was! The complimentary artwork is superb and the poetry is mesmerizing. It's a MUST READ!

Here are some other easy ways to help:

- Tell your colleagues and friends about this book; talk it up over coffee, during phone conversations, at gatherings, etc.
- Order a copy of the book for a friend.
- Post an honest review of this book on Amazon.
- Use this book as a book study with a small poetry or reading club.

And, thank you for your support!

ABOUT KRISTEN CLARK

I am a lover of all things beautiful, and this book was a natural next step after publishing my butterfly poetry book and bird poetry book.

Butterflies, birds, flowers, you name it and I love it. And my goal with this book is simply to celebrate the beauty and unique nature of flowers and the poetic language and art forms they have inspired over the years.

When I'm not compiling and publishing poetry books, I'm working on my next book in the *Women of Worth* book series, featuring inspirational short stories written by Christian women celebrating their journeys of adversity and overcoming. Inspired by my experience as a story contributor for *Chicken Soup for the Soul* book series and the results of my award-winning book, *Becoming a Woman of Worth: Creating a More Confident You*, it is my heart's desire to help women everywhere build confidence as a spiritual mindset by learning to see themselves as God sees them.

I'm also an editor and publisher with a huge heart for helping others write and publish their story or poetry. For more information on our publishing services, visit www.AmericanMuttPress.com.

Finally, I live in Houston with my darling husband, Lawrence, who is a writer, speaker, musician, and university professor.

For more information about my other passions, please feel free to visit:

- www.AllThingsButterflies.com
- www.BackyardBirdingParadise.com
- www.AmericanMuttPress.com
- www.HisSideoftheLookingGlass.com
- www.BecomingaWomanofWorth.com
- www.LivingwithGratitude.com
- www.KristenClark.org

30 CLASSIC AND VINTAGE POEMS ABOUT BUTTERFLIES
With Full-Color Photographs

By Kristen Clark

Available on Amazon.com and Barnesandnoble.com

KRISTEN CLARK

BACKYARD BIRDS & THE POETS WHO LOVED THEM
With Full-Color Photographs

By Kristen Clark

Available on Amazon.com and BarnesandNoble.com

www.ingramcontent.com/pod-product-compliance
Lightning Source LLC
Chambersburg PA
CBHW042313150426
43200CB00001B/5